A Late Disorder

A Late Disorder

Poems
by
Ben Greer

 Bay Oak Publishers, Ltd.

by
Ben Greer

A Late Disorder
ISBN 978-0-9741713-8-8
Manufactured in the United States of America

This is for George and Susan Garrett who filled my rotten teeth and bought me clothes and fed me and taught me how to live. Every day I think of you.

BG

Acknowledgements

The Southern Review: **James Dickey's Lot, Beneath a Yankee Bridge**

The South Carolina Review: **James Dickey's Last Assignment, Terminal, The Annual Physical, Old Blood**

Georgetown Review: **Glue**

The Texas Review: **Rhapsody**

Main Channel Voices: **This New Town**

The James Dickey Newsletter: **Completion**

Elvis in Oz, The University of Virginia Press: **Providence**

The Southern Poetry Anthology: **A Teacher's Discovery, Death Among Friends**

Runes, a Review of Poetry: **Plant**

Winning Writers Online: **Churchill's Contrition, Breaking the Curfew**

Contents

For the World   10

    12

Reunion   13
Seasons of the Killer   14
This New Town   15
Rhapsody   16
Less   17
Madam Curie's Notebooks   18
Death Among Friends   19
Completion   20
Duet   21
The Wind in May   22
Preservation of the Species   23
Old Blood   24
Three Cywydds   25
    Southern Snow
    January Joy
    James Dickey's Last Assignment
Tsunami, Christmas, 2004   28
Johnny Drummer   29
Reoccurrence   31
Prelude   32
Chaplain FDNY   33

The Cry of Tin   34
Breaking the Curfew   35
Glue   36
The Fever in Soweto   37
Churchill's Contrition   38
Providence   39
Below   40
A Pornographer's Lament   41
Viagra   42
Balmoral Dreaming   43
Te Deum   44
Nocturne   45
Beneath a Yankee Bridge   47
A Teacher's Discovery   48
Prayer from a Beauty   49
A Little Joy   50
The Annual Physical   51
Starry Men   52
The Lovely Prescription   53
James Dickey's Lot   54
Apology to Winnie   56
Death of a Novelist   57
Melodrama   58
Couple Dies in Plane Crash   59
A Poem for Abagail   60

For the World

I didn't hear them when they died
but I thought I felt something.
It was raining, a February
day as I sat in my office
watching the local news.
The announcer said they hit
the side wall of the building.
Calls were made to appropriate
experts. No one seemed to know
why. Immediately I thought
it has to be the black glass wall.
Somehow they could not see it.
But then there was the other thing
I knew and that I had known
since I was a boy. They were drunk
from the glistening red berries:
pyracantha grown winter fat.

I crossed the street where the dark
hospital stood. It looked as if
someone had thrown red roses
by the dozens against the glass—
a hundred cardinals lay shattered
in a blur. Some of them not dead,
feathers and wings trembling, broken
beaks agape in their freezing
bacchanal. Beneath umbrellas
a crowd stared at the agony.
I knew no one could do anything
to anesthetize this pain.

At home, I found the secret box
where I kept them in a row.
I had many, each wrapped in
a silken sheath. Each as perfect
as any pure edge could be.

It was an old idea which
grew around the age of sex
that if I cut myself until
the blood ran down in warm ribbons
all other pain would lessen. All—
not just my own. The very
pain of the world would diminish
into balls of red cotton
which I hid beneath my bed.
Sleeping above the crimson host
I dreamed of healing
a million wounds.

Now I open the little silks
and slide the clear edge of razor
against this belly for the world.

                    For Kwame Dawes

It looked much better than this. Some artist drew it
the way they do with lines that are never straight
and curves that have something else in them like
breath, or some inscrutable motion.
On a cement wall it was yellow for the trunk,
green for the canopy and even a brown knot
whirling in a lovely way which seemed without
effort. Beneath this tree was one word, stamped,
not written, in black: PLANT.
I drew up close thinking it was a definition,
only to realize that it was not that at all—
it was a command. Plant! Go plant! An injunction
to the world. To all who are green. To all who are not
green. To me.
I smiled the whole day
filling the earth with forests.

Reunion

Since it is formal
I prepare for my
visit with proper clothes:
sweats and stocking cap
white socks and black gloves.

Arriving, I punch play.
Rocky vibrates their stones,
sends black crows away
while above my head
I lift my gloved hands

Triumphantly. I dance
across their red clay bones,
the golden wedding rings
and plastic teeth, singing
my own victory:

Dead. Dead. All of you dead
deep in the skinny red earth
and me as fat as
a butter fed cat
beyond the reach of your hurt.

Seasons of the Killer

To murder in Spring
takes very little courage:
life is abundant.

June is my illness.
The terrible heat slows me.
I hide from the sun.

Leaves yellow and fall
into piles of fragile death.
I hunt in the cold.

The winter moon smiles
having seen me. Is she dead?
I hold her white face.

This New Town

Guiltily, I have come out to see you
waving in the sea fog, a big blue fir.
To make a new friend, I agreed to order
a chainsaw and cut you down for his view.

All night long, I hear you begging the wind
to come and say something magical.
To produce some enchanted madrigal,
hoping to wake my green conscience, rescind

My offer. I've always loved any tree
like some member of my family.
By sunrise guilt deepens into despair.

I wish not to offend this new neighbor,
in this new town, but cutting you I abhor.
What to do? Send this poem, and hope he'll care?

Rhapsody

You do not think about the animals.
You say it always makes you sad.
You do not consider their stoic eyes,
The soft drawings of their breath,
Their kindness which is not the world's.
You sleep and let the others beat
Open the cells of the guiltless.
But should something catch you
Unaware and reveal a mother
Slaughtered before her calf—
Weep. In the waking of your soul
Weep and rise and follow the drum.

Less

Deference is one of them we must learn—
the bleak graces of middle-age. Mostly
vigorous, we boomers blanch before
the ineluctable diminution:

Piecemeal we lose our health. The eyes go first
my mother said, round as an apple dumpling
and the same color, after quadruple
bypass. For years I wondered how she breathed.

And yes, my eyes did go first: bifocals.
This was nothing. A magnifying glass
would have worked as well as thousand dollar
tortoise shell specs. What came later was real

Horror. Something bloating an artery.
A blockage the cardiologist smiled,
angioplasty should take care of it.
Afterwards, less fat, less sugar, less booze.

Less. The long surrender has begun.
There are some who will not. They will die.
So will we, but later, if we let go
carefully.

Madam Curie's Notebooks

In lead-lined boxes to properly shield us
your notebooks lay, their vigor still unquelled.
Some say they glow. Have any pages held
literally the power to kill? We can fuss

With diction all day, but your books will rot flesh
from the bones of anyone who reads them.
To know that my words could actually condemn
my gentle reader, snatch away the fresh

Lust of pretty eyes, deplete the full breath—
oh, God, I would risk eternal death
to deliver such a catastrophe

With only words. So now you think I'm insane—
most of you, but not the writers who remain
wild to leave some incandescent legacy.

Death Among Friends

Now is the dread inception of your mortal end.
For years I worried about this very moment—
about who would first hear the physician's comment:
I'm sorry. It's cancer. Are you her friend?

Afterwards, I drove around for half the day.
Then something else inexplicable: a brown
cloud descended. I felt as if I might drown
in the strange, sudden stench. Wild fires burning in May.

I was surprised to be so completely shaken.
I am sixty, seasoned, but was mistaken
to think that I could calmly accept the news

and balance my checkbook or workout or day dream
about anything. Brown and still, the gripping hours teem
with pictures of you, of me, of all we will lose.

For Marsha

Completion

Fall is our best fire.
This October we build it
exuberantly.

So, since I still am
I lift up and search for them.
Below, something moves.

The kids want it big
so they can remember it
as the perfect one.

Gratefully I fly,
my soft eyes burning the night
towards the leaping thing.

The moth dives down fast
and pops, sizzles in the flames.
It makes us all sad.

                      Here is the moment
I am become beautiful
in the heat of men.

Duet

Your life mask I keep before me,
but not at the center of my desk.
It sits beside a box of paper
scraps, the pieces spotted with ink:
words trying to become

Something. Since I hate things not balanced
I sometimes move it to the proper place—
right in the clutter of my work,
but I cannot leave it here
even for a while.

I push it again to the side,
put your wry aluminum face
in eraser dust and shavings,
thinking: how silly, we are finished
you and I.

The Wind in May

In May I start to enter late
and slow beneath the oaks,
to watch wind shake the leaves
and to listen to it rattle slate
of houses near the campus.

I stay as long as I can keep
my waiting low, not obvious,
as if I'm happy with the Spring.
I cough to prove I'm not asleep,
just pausing here before I go

To class and final duties there.
I call the roll, but do not look;
I make my voice sound light with ease
for through the years I've learned to bear
this departure deceptively.

After you have left the room,
I remain and hear your voices,
laughing down the hollow stairs.
The wind in May presages gloom.

Preservation of the Species

So pornography has become your obsession
since the oncologist gave you a month to six.
I am shocked. Preparing to cross the sleepy Styx
you should have planted a green seed in the sun;

or started another afghan—more like you.
They say to obsess while waiting is usual,
but all those teenagers writhing in sexual
acrobatics. Perhaps dying creates a new

libido. Suddenly I remember a fish
black and silver in my hands; it came in anguish
and came again, never stopping until the end

of its dim life. Is this why sex fascinates you?
Is this why you rage when I flip to a milieu
more appropriate? Was your life so cold, my friend?

Old Blood

The white roses on my mantle open
a view of my new life: a thrombosis,
near death, then a nineteen-year-old heart
cut from the chest of a boy.

I never expected sickness so soon.
My blood lived their best years beyond eighty,
after they had rid themselves of bourbon
and vanity. Could they think me

Anything but weak, an experience
which they kept at bay their mottled lives long.
I will not think of their triumphant
wellness, but the less-lived boy who,

Like me (though much younger) was frailty.
Something soft bursting in his cerebrum
sent me my immaculate heart because
he signed on the bleak paper: *Give,*

Harvest all that remains, all that is good,
to someone not come to such early death.
You, my old blood, my family, would not
see his selfless business as strength

But proof of an inferiority.
Still this youthful act allows me
to challenge your hegemony in flesh.
May his will perpetuate me.

Three Cywydds

Southern Snow

The small snow of winter descends
and the magnolia apprehends
the truth: it bends with cold grace
for this frozen falling is rare,
will vanish with sun into air
leaving no care or harsh trace.

January Joy

Bring me the January rain.
Let no leaf of summer remain,
no sun constrain the deluge.
For nothing grows without the gloom
of soft downpours outside my room.
All my springs loom bright and huge.

James Dickey's Last Assignment

"Now write me some immortal line."
Though lasting words could not be mine,
it was a fine instruction.
I knew this last assignment told
me much about your end: behold
the poet's cold submission.

Tsunami, Christmas, 2004

Those of us who had decided
to believe in them shuddered.
Two hundred-fifty thousand dead?
Because of a shift down deep,
then a wrinkle of blue water
silent as the last edge of
atmosphere above
rolled across the flat
Pacific plains to kill them all
with a crush of starfish, coral
and delicate shells. Camus said:
if we cared, we had to choose
either miracles or absurdity.
What horror now it is to try
to embrace all which is luminous.
How do we explain to the others?
How do we explain to ourselves?
Mystery is too easy.
Rejection is despair
beyond the repairing.

Johnny Drummer

Most of us caught things in the woods when we were boys:
terrapins and spiders, minnows and butterflies,
even wiggly earthworms which we kept in shoeboxes
filled with black, wet dirt. Most of us let them go, or
traded them among ourselves. He was not this way.

All the little life of his fields Johhny killed and
preserved in various kinds of jars. The glasses
held red newts, columns of round turtles,
long lizard links, spotted green frogs, and insects
by the hundreds: bees, grubs, wasps, folded mantises.

These creatures, these little souls made immortal
in formalin were the happiest collections
he put up. Things began to change. Parents became
monsters. Sweet dogs and cats were obliterated
on the road. The other collecting began when
Johnny found his mother was a man.

First his tonsils—a normal evisceration
from his teen body. Then a little finger
cut off with a hatchet while splitting wood.
Appendicitis filled him with a deeper
joy, then sorrow. The doctor would not let him keep

it. This denial of his flesh allowed him to
explode into his full blown self: he needed faces—
palpable, intelligent faces to wince and weep,

to articulate the beautiful asymmetry
of his work. The doctor's son was a natural

choice—both revenge and experiment. Since
they were friends, taking him in the woods was easy.
A handful of glittering quartz to his skill brought
messy death, then careful butchery. Johnny
set two pieces in a bubbling aquarium:

five gallons of alcohol held a head and heart.
The rest he studied. Doodling the Isle of Langerhans
he remembered Durher and Buonarotti.
Leonardo lunching among the corpses.
He went to college. Campus was laughing with flesh
and epiphany—by their parts he would know them.

Reoccurrence

Bust out the morphine and the Tattinger,
tap the Demerol and chill the Mumms.
Liberate the chocolates from their tinsel nests,
sauce the pork and free bourbon from the drums.

Let the long anticipated party
begin. Invite the dour oncologists
who were sure I would die their tedious
death of chemotherapy. Nope. My wrists

Remain pale and soft and inviolate.
Strong enough to pop a cork, or whip cream
so thick that strawberries bounce and glitter.
I drink. I laugh. I eat. Death is a dream.

Prelude

September is blue, impossibly so.
At Montauk the brown beaches are bare.
In the Hamptons the palaces empty
into Eighty-fourth Street and Park:
the City busies itself again.

Beneath floor 100 in North Tower's sway
traders pour another black cup, their eyes
full of geese flying south and the blueberry
Atlantic, quiet in the turning time.

Beyond the Hudson, we lose ourselves in Fall:
the books of children, the apparel, ball—
the warm, last days before Thanksgiving
and the rest, while a plane sweeps across
the sleepy republic towards a time
when many must become extraordinary.

Chaplain FDNY

Father Judge lies dead upon the white altar
of St. Paul's Church, placed here by firemen
for whom his gin eyes were always full of prayer.
Stretched out in ashes in his last amen,

He does not seem dead, but rather puzzled
at the interruption of his work:
    Is this some dream bed, or me passed out on
the altar saying the Mass too long?

My heart failing me, and the boys sticking
me here before the Tabernacle in
a true honor? He stops. Smoking sheets
are borne into the church. He remembers:

        I see them again. They jump. They hold
each others' hands, furiously
striking the street, men and women.
What rain is this that falls in human flesh?

He awakes, rising, stepping towards corpses,
hands searching sooty pockets for Holy oil.
Softly applying it to skin which remains
he whispers: "Nunc dimittis, Domine…"

The Cry of Tin

When even elements grieve with rending,
I think all existence holds a sorrow
that we cannot escape until the ending
of this life's persistence. Chemists call it

"The cry of tin" when they bend a piece
and the soft metal whines like some pet
who in our power adores, though we crease
its small soul which inclines towards us still.

Everything connects (animate and not)
in the occupation we call being, but
how I wish we could somehow change the plot,
make our long submissions work without agony.

Breaking the Curfew

In the markets of Jenin, bread is soggy with their blood—
children so small they fluttered through tents of honey and
fruit.
Hidden in caves a week, they were completely dissolute
with sunlight and the breeze of the desert. Until a scud

Blew up and the carnivorous bullets of machine guns
scattered and drove them again to their holes, all but a few.
Henan, why didn't you grab what you could and
rendezvous
in some subterranean oasis with your loved ones?

Now you lie here among the other shattered vessels,
holding your arms around a brown loaf. No one wrestles
it from you. None of your friends. Their arms are full and
still too.

Like a falling of butterflies, the children lie dead.
Let the politicians walk this street of blood and bread
to see if they will still insist: how meet is war and true.

Glue

May is my disintegration.
The classroom holds only light
and the gloom that summer brings:
empty buildings, empty life.

My very person shows the change—
ink of essays fades away
from my lessoned fingertips, while
my clothes deteriorate

To greasy t-shirts, riven pants.
Soon I do not bathe or brush;
it is too much to clean my nails
or cut my burgeoning beard.

A campus cop asks who I am.
"Tomatoes," I would like to say
but my woes he could never see,
nor the cure in my garden

Planted in Spring. Tall and sunny,
young and trim, the tomato vines
slow my grim dissolution.
I disappear among them,

Until the last of summer haze
when my students start oozing in.
The young glue sticks me together,
and I am I again.

The Fever in Soweto

Sex with a virgin will cure you of AIDS
the infected say in South Africa.
Children, do not play beyond your parents'
eyes: the thin man is hunting tonight.

Where did he find you, little Tombi?
Were you dancing beneath the Baobab?
Or catching a bee to throw at your friends?
Though only nine, the skeleton took you

Out of childhood into his dread disease.
Sweating with fever, tens of thousands pray
us to deliver the bright cocktail,
but the Minister of Health forbids it.

Her words: "Too much money. Unproven."
Sometimes even the oppressed are guilty.
Run like wind, Tombi, gazelles will comfort
you in the wandering softness of herds.

And what of us, in our cool opulence?
Will we withdraw, sour with spells and darkness?
We should grieve each hour for a solution—
or plead: Mandela, Mandela, Mandela.

2001

Churchill's Contrition

Bethlehem, now I hear you weeping
in the Church of the Nativity:
the steeple gunfire rules the city
and mocks the sound of bells keeping

The holy hours. If such terror can
invade this sacred darkness where light
supposedly was born, then no might
may resist it, no fortress of man.

And yet it was my own endeavor,
justice, that made this land forever
a place of evisceration.

Bethlehem, you have a bloody scent.
Oh little town, should I now repent
my careful theft to build a nation?

Providence

I like to learn the way of things
how they fit or break apart
how a bit tears into steel;
the glory of a lock.

I like to learn the way of things
and not just the tool and die
but how a bass fans out a nest
how a man will die—

Then live

To fly on rainbow wings
and sail beyond the dark
as if it were a certainty
that the way of things is art.

Below

Now
I move
stealthily
behind my house,
studying the ground
deep in summer debris:
avalanches of leaves dry
in the turning light. Out West Fall
broods softly in the great yellow plains
where the temperature tries to reach forty.
Some creatures are digging in my backyard. They
push up beach sand which balances like white castles
across the grass. Something else is making perfect holes
beside the sharp holly. Though I cannot catch the diggers
in their secret industry, the magic work makes me feel glad.

A Pornographer's Lament

Let all my good words beg apology
for the other ones gone bad
which scratched or dug into the page sins
that might compel a boy
to dream some lusciousness: like
catching some brown beauty in ecstasy
before her image in a stream
and from behind taking her fiercely
as he reads in his bed
my words by light beneath a quilt.

I should make them praise beautifully
the one and only voice I know
to make the blacker parts of print light
but words refuse to go
like me any way but their own.

Viagra

Astonished
I lie beneath
the sudden tent of sheet
and ask you to come here

now.

Balmoral Dreaming

I threw a hand of lilacs
at Boris Yeltsin's feet
and climbed a tank beside him
all Moscow filled the street.

With hammer, pick and shovel
despite the Stazi's bawl
I drank champagne with comrades
before we blew the Wall.

Around the world and further
inside the square Beijing
we raised a paper Princess
convulsing Deng Xiaoping.

But all this lovely grandeur
burns solely in my head;
at fifty-three and balding
I'll probably end up dead

Before I break one dreaming
apart from all the rest
and sew it on my shoulder
or pin it to my chest.

But dreaming holds the way for me.
I'm far too old to quarrel,
besides I've seen the evening news—
there's trouble in Balmoral.

Te Deum

When I was brimming at the lip
for you, any sleight beauty
would spill me over: a white gate
wide open, the fibrillation
and shimmer of deep minnows,
a daisy gold in two petals,
the taste of M&M's in one
mouthful, than guzzled down with
popping Coke. Any of these things
and a million others would make
my adolescent self shout out
thanksgivings to you, God. Bring me
to that effervescence once more
until I boil and empty
into inexhaustible depths.

Nocturne

I write these lines to answer your aubade
though really light and morning should belong
to me to keep my logic pure as lauds.
You see I have chosen to whistle long
and loud to block out death which constantly
affects the minds of guys like you and me.
You bet I wonder too about the time
when time is up and we begin a fresh
trajectory outside this flesh.
I'm thinking: death like birth becomes sublime.

I lie down late in the afternoon
and watch the last of winter light press through
my bedroom shade. I wake to find the moon
against the night and stars which I construe
to be a distant smile as we below
begin to end our day within the glow
of icy booze or sugar treats or meals.
Shadows are not the end, but rather scenes
among a billion more that play between
night and day our space conceals.

Slowly night strengthens, and dreams replace
the manic stuttering of consciousness
we children learned to lose without a trace
of fear as long as parents stayed to bless
and hold until we made our way into
a dappled field of light where all was new.
If we believe and make ourselves a kid
again—all tiptoe with possibility

and hope which age so shrilly
condemns—we could seek and make a bid

On that lovely field, and advancing find
all we have lost or dreamed or wanted so.
Philip, I wish I could have teased your mind
and said there was another way to know.
I doubt you would have listened very well.
You loved despair and made your mind a hell.
I step into the dark almost complete.
Beside the curb, the paperboy unfolds
the news, not knowing what it holds.
I wave goodnight and whistle down the street.

Beneath a Yankee Bridge

The day you heard it, we were drunk
and bleeding from our soles,
shooting hoops beside your house
barefoot for some reason.
I'm sure it was the booze
that numbed our feet to ooze
upon the cement.

The call came from some northern state,
and Maxine held the phone
staring at our wounded feet
so bloody were the prints.
It's something bad, she slurred
as you embraced the words:
"his head busted the ice."

I recall the simplicity—
you bared your gappy teeth
and flicked your tongue across them
relishing response,
then said to me cold as lead
"John Berryman is dead
beneath a Yankee bridge."

What followed then I can't forget,
a cheerful cruelty:
"W.B. Yeats of dead Swinburne said—
'And now I'm king of cats.'"
Just twenty-one, I sat
learning the trade.

A Teacher's Discovery

I would not let you fall in love with me
though you wanted to because of what I found:
music. The craze and crack of your words
I read that winter morning I will always
hear. And because I told you: look,
look at this. Look at what you have done.
Incredible. Your hands grabbed mine and brought
them to your mouth wet as half a peach
to kiss, knowing the agonies
of your life now had meaning: a poem
with such incomprehensible edge
that all who press it open and bleed
at last understanding their own sickness,
spilling it out luxuriously,
pouring it out hotly, madly, dreamily
until there is only one sense remaining:
the emptiness of the healed.

Prayer from a Beauty

Make me into a marsupial:
a bandicoot would do.
Pour me a long slouch of belly
and dim my blue eyes too.

Soften my angular cheekbones
and let them go to fat.
Sprinkle my rosy flesh with hair.
My dimples fill so that

lovers no longer desire to touch
or hold me in their arms.
Render all my manifestations
of beauty and my charm

down to a surly ugliness
and then no one will try
intimacy with this brittle self
who only wants to die.

A Little Joy

In October, in the Whole Foods store, I'm not happy.
All the summer vegetables are flat and brown.
They remind me of me. Rotting. Out of
season. 58 now. I made my share of sweet mistakes:
booze and pierced lovers and oodles of valium.
But for decades my sprouts were insecticideless
and I never ate cheeseburgers, though I dreamed
of them: opalescent slices of onion
and tomato and prickly lettuce. I love
to dream about the things I cannot have.
I know why. So do you. But who would invent
such frustration? Some of us know, but
most of us do not care.

All this makes me sad beneath
the sad lights of the Whole Foods store.
The cashier totals me up. I look
down at the meter. It says Approved!
I look at it a little longer.
Well, yes, okay. Approved! Take it.
Go on. There it is—a little joy.
Seize it when it comes your way.

The Annual Physical

In that hard room
we will all arrive
ineluctably.
We have noticed something:

A pain which persists;
a stippled bump;
shaking in a hand;
notes without melody.

Those previous vials
of warm vermilion
liberated us
from the fear of death

And we celebrated:
a mirror of white lines,
glistening doughnuts,
a triple scotch neat,
hot pornography.

All these celebrations
are now forgotten.
The tests were not good.
Incarceration
begins for us today.

We have entered the cell
and the disease
awaits our response.

Starry Men

Bloody toothpicks in my pocket
more than remind me of you—
it is you, this habit, picking
at my gums after meals, though
I think your digging was not
cleanliness, but something darker:
always you hurt yourself, Daddy.
Usually more deeply, carving
your bony legs with little stars
and letting me count them until
I cut them too: meteors
falling from my knees to ankles
made me feel I could anesthetize
my life.

It took us a long time to know
a hard truth: the world will not abate
for starry men its agitation
no matter how diligently
we whittle our gentle flesh
hoping by small cuts to make
the big ones bearable.

The Lovely Prescription

It seemed always in the summer
I would take my grandfather's
warm black book. Soft as the flesh
of his hands, and sit beneath
a menthol of green leaves
reading the underlined words
he preached on Sunday.

Scripture was my remission
from the abuse of my parents,
the craze of my halfborn heart,
the overwhelming apprehension
life was something about to burst.

In those medicinal afternoons
I was relieved of all these fears,
assuaged by ancient miracles:
David and his little sling;
Daniel lounging among the cats;
Shadrak, Meshak, and Abednego.

So now when things feel ominous,
I take off walking to the woods,
holding that soft and heavy book,
reading again those Sunday stories,
letting leaves fill this lovely prescription.

James Dickey's Lot

> Only the written word remains.
> —Horace

So I will start with the end:
staring at lights on water,
a dock that will not give
beneath your feet again.

Of your time there is not one
thing left here, not one gray brick
of the narrow, low house
at whose roof I for fun

Dared to throw rocks, a boy
in love with poetry.

Or was it for fame I threw?
You were truly famous then,
all the critics agree.
My raw intellect knew

The answer to your question:
"Because I love symmetry,"
I said, and saw you smile
at awkward deception.

Back then I did not know
deception was your truth

And became mine for long years,
allowing us to spar in
perfect syncopation
through football, class, and beers.

Now beneath the owl-held tree
you lie deep in root light,
while standing on your lot
staring is only me

Stricken by the ancient line:
Littera scripta manet.

Apology to Winnie

I have hurt you more
than my mother
who deserved all the pain
which a healthy soul
could give. My sweet dog
you suffer my violence,
you bear my fist blows
for a woman who fucked
me in every way
including flesh, and lived
a fine old life not given
even to saints.

Death of a Novelist

At last there is no hope.
No one will throw flowers.
No one will offer millions
and introduce Spielberg
at a Malibu hideaway
where a citrus girl and boy
offer themselves for inspection.
Here there are only words—
quick, mean, clear words
which will not applaud,
but only give themselves
like bright Easter communion
hoping to make you pure.

Melodrama

Happy and young in the craft
you did not need or want
the damp applause of others.
You hated notice, prided yourself
in the loneliness of blind work.

How splendid it felt to be small
and violent as a seed.
Your little will burned brightly
in the vastness of obscurity.
Sometimes you yelled to the depths:
Cover me up. Cover me up.
Heap all you can on me. Nothing
will be enough to bury what I have
or what I will come to be.

Now all that sureness has been
ground away by terrible events:
your mother's druggy suicide
which is becoming your own,
your father's murder discovered late,
cancer, the collapse of
secret hopes. All this leaving
you with only one clear thought:

Melodrama is all that's left.

Couple Dies in Plane Crash

I throw the yellow roses from your birthday
in the backyard where the young deer have lain
through these cold Yankee nights. The grass is long
because we did not let the boy cut it
and all summer in the mornings it was flat
and white because of their sleeping. Yellow
roses on white grass is pretty, but it
makes me uneasy to do this. I should keep them
even though we are leaving Maine today
on the plane for home. You say it doesn't
matter, but both of us feel that it does,
as if throwing away something so
delicate, so much a part of this special
day might curse you or us. We do not believe
in superstitions except in the greatest
one of all, but we stand and stare until
we cannot bear it and I gather
them up and come inside rolling them
in wax paper through which a thorn sticks me
drawing blood. One drop splatters across
these faces hidden in their thin missile.
Carefully, I wipe it off packing
the delicate roll in my suitcase.
We hold one another and feel as though
something has been avoided.

A Poem for Abagail

When you think of me
think of the wind
in the trees, dropping
down across wild
roses beside the drive,
leading to the sea
and Indian Island
where your Mom
and I saw the tough lady
with her kids brown
as the rough beach, let out
by the public ferry
as if she owned it,
then gunned her little car
up the shore throwing sand
to the wind pushing through
the salty woods,
the wind always going
a different way,
either empty or not,
full or not,
sometimes moody,
hissing, thunderous, silly,
but always skating
through obstacles standing
before it, as if
at play and by playing
accomplishing
everything
for you.

About the Author

A Late Disorder is Ben Greer's first published collection of poetry. A native of South Carolina, he has written and published five novels. *Slammer*, his first novel, is based on his experiences working in a maximum security prison. His latest novel, *Murder in the Holy City*, is the first in the Archibald Sims detective series set in Charleston. Greer teaches at the University of South Carolina and is working on his next Sims novel.

About the Author

Ben Greer's first novel, *Slammer*, is based on his experiences working in a maximum security prison. Greer has since written and published four other novels. His latest novel, *Murder in the Holy City*, is the first in the Archibald Sims detective series set in Charleston. Greer teaches at the University of South Carolina and is working on his next Sims novel. This is his first published collection of poems.